D1796401

BONJOUR, BETTÉ-LU

by

Countess Ghirelli

DORRANCE & COMPANY

Philadelphia

To my mother,
Florence Anthony Sanson,
the kindest person I've ever known.

BONJOUR, BETTÉ-LU

As these lines are being written, Betté-lu has risen to the status of an international cat in our old and stately community of Chestnut Hill, having acquired the manners of a charming lady whose savoir-faire matches that of the south of France. We who are the members of her immediate family see that her attitude has definitely changed after having spent the winter on the French Riviera.

The story of Betté-lu really begins in 1964, when the little lady was a kitten. She belongs to Grandfather, who acquired her unintentionally at Pastorius Park, where he used to pay visits to feed the squirrels. Certainly there was a strong attraction on both sides, and as the years have passed we realize nothing can part them—not even the Atlantic Ocean. Discovering that she was an orphan, Grandfather, a compassionate man towards animals, brought Betté-lu to live at our house.

I had nothing against cats, but at first I was strongly inclined to disapprove of the newcomer because of my poodle, Pepper. Perhaps I was prejudiced, but I thought he was the most wonderful pet in the world. His fur was jet black and soft as silk, and there was a rich chocolate color to his brown eyes. A true aristocrat, dignity enhanced Pepper's every gesture. Certainly there was nothing animal in his manners. To those of us who loved him, the gentlemanly manners that seemed all-important to him stood out clearly.

For the record, Pepper, whose real name was Bijou, began his life at Cap Ferrat in the south of France in 1953 and was purchased for me by my husband's grandmother, the Comtesse de Valbranca, who lived in Nice. Her American grandfather was Isaac Skinner Waterman of Chestnut Hill

Pepper: Sometimes I'd call him "le Marquis de Poivre." After all, everyone else had a title in the family.

(noted financier and landowner), and since I was from Chestnut Hill, she seemed to enjoy granting me my every wish—and one was to own a real French poodle.

At just this time she and I discovered Pepper, curled up in a cage asleep at the Monte Carlo International Dog Exhibition. His mother, a descendant of eight champions, was being shown, and she later took first prize.

As Pepper matured and we travelled annually back and forth between Nice and Philadelphia, I gradually realized I had acquired not a dog but a person—a friend and confidante who sensed my happiness, joy and sadness. Sometimes I'd call him "le Marquis de Poivre," which at first shocked the grandmothers. But after all, everyone else in the family had a title.

His loyalty was never once doubted. I was first in his heart, and certainly he expected a similar loyalty in return.

The afternoon Betté-lu arrived at our house, Pepper stood motionless for several moments. He peered down at her. His tail never wavered. Then he turned, and his chocolate brown eyes blinked at me sorrowfully, as though I had been unfaithful, unworthy of his devotion through these many years. So I quickly moved closer to him and stroked his pompom head, assuring him of my affection. After all, here was a middle-aged gentleman suddenly feeling jealous—old and tired compared to the new pet, a young and dainty creature, friendly and uninhibited by a cruel and sophisticated world. (If anyone knows about astrology, Pepper was born under the sign of Cancer, with his moon in Taurus.)

Giving attention to another playmate was the worst offense I could commit against this sensitive, soft-natured gentleman. He was no fighter; he wouldn't attempt to compete with her or anyone. His sadness frightened us badly and made us determined to make a fuss over him as well as the kitten.

Meanwhile, Betté-lu leaped up and down restlessly, and gradually she crept closer, then closer still.

Finally, Pepper growled, and the kitten backed up, somewhat shocked at the dog's protest. She crouched nonplussed alongside of Grandfather's shoe.

Admittedly, I knew nothing about cats and their behavior. I had no idea how Betté-lu and Pepper would react alone, and I wanted no battle, no eyes scratched out, no bloody wounds—

no Waterloo. Rightly or wrongly, I insisted they live apart as much as possible.

As it turned out, a firm hand was needed with Grandfather, too, who thought the whole thing was a big joke, and daily he would playfully tease the two pets.

However, odd though it may seem, in less than a week the pets shared the same bowl. The dignified black head bent down, if a trifle condescendingly, beside the little kitten plowing into her meal.

My mother's maternal instinct proved a help in many ways. She'd cuddle the kitten and stroke Pepper's pompom at the same time, telling him that Betté-lu was just a baby, and it was up to him to protect her. He seemed to understand.

In another week they snuggled close together when they slept, which I'd never have believed if I hadn't seen them myself.

Thereafter, the pets were inseparable, and Pepper assumed a paternal relationship with the little orphan. While I spoke only in French to Pepper and in English to Betté-lu, the latter always seemed to understand our conversation.

When I was at home Pepper spent a lot of his time with me, and now Betté-lu joined us too. I found I had to make room for the three of us wherever I sat.

In three years Betté-lu matured and enjoyed all the assets of our lovely garden. She became a cat of strength and strong will, but graceful and very pretty. The fur on Betté-lu's back is a delicately blended mixture of black, brown and gray. Her chest and stomach and most of her face are covered in silky white fur that she keeps spotless. Lithe and slender, she moves and sits with a sureness and serenity that human beings can envy.

But in those three years, Pepper grew older and slower. And finally, just before his fifteenth birthday, he became ill.

For several days he wouldn't eat, and he seemed listless. Our veterinarian diagnosed a tumor in his throat and said that an operation at his age would be impossible.

When we finally lost Pepper, all of us became ill. And in the days following, even Betté-lu would only pick at her food. She had known, I think, that something was wrong. When Pepper lay ill she approached him without her customary playfulness. She would settle herself gently beside him and look at him for long periods of time.

I wrapped and carried him myself to his favorite corner of the garden, where he used to stand—bright-eyed and every inch alive—gazing through the fence at the neighbor's pony. His grave is now a pretty shrine with lovely rocks and English ivy circling it. A lily grows in the center and forget-me-nots bloom at his feet.

Often Betté-lu can be seen perched on a rock near him, and I sometimes think she's talking to him, as I often do when I pass by that corner.

That summer I felt Betté-lu had been sent to us to make life easier after Pepper had gone. This thought kept us all going; for it was almost impossible even to mention his name without lumps forming in our throats. Those of you who have lost favorite dogs need no further explanation.

Three months later I paid a return visit to Nice—for the first time without Pepper. The reunion of all the family and friends was not the same.

My heart ached, seeing his favorite romping grounds on the far end of the cliff at my villa at Cap Ferrat. And now even the grandmother who had given Pepper to me was gone and so was my mother-in-law. It was a little too much for me that winter, and I came back to America sorrowfully when spring came.

When I arrived home, the sight of Betté-lu comforted me. I never thought I'd see the day when a cat could lift my spirits.

As I opened the luggage, she climbed into a suitcase and curled up there, watching me intently as I unpacked. And for the rest of the day as I went about the house, she spent most of her time with me—far more than she had done previously.

We became friends, fast friends, and within a short time I lost my heart to the little cat and enjoyed having her as a close companion. As a result of this friendship I learned the habits of cats—their cautiousness, shrewdness and patience. And she taught me many things valuable to human beings.

It was the following fall that the family sailed on the *Michaelangelo* to spend a year on the French Riviera. The family physician had advised them not to endure another cold and snowy winter in their autumn years. The year before they hadn't even been able to walk on the glazed sidewalks. The fear of losing their footing frightened them even more than the thoughts of a cold or the flu.

To prevent me from loneliness, Betté-lu remained with me to look after the house. Within a month a pleading letter came, asking me to bring the cat with me if at all possible, instead of putting her in a kennel when I flew over for the Christmas holidays.

Grandfather missed his playmate, and with all the cats to be found in France he wanted Betté-lu.

Dutiful offspring that I try to be, I arranged to take the cat with me. Naturally, when my friends learned of it, Betté-lu took on a more glamorous look and suddenly became the envy of everyone. Here was a cat (?!) going abroad to spend the winter on the French Riviera.

A few days later I arranged for my flight to Nice via London, because I had already planned a stop-over there to visit my brother Allan and his family, whom I hadn't seen in two years.

The airline office instructed me that all cats going to England were to have a physical check-up not more than forty-eight hours prior to flight-time, and a vet's certificate of health. She would be considered "in transit" enroute to France, with only a stop-over in London. Otherwise, she'd be quarantined for six months—England's strict ruling on all animals. The ticket agent also informed me that they allow only two animals on each flight, one in cargo and one in the passenger section. Fortunately Betté-lu's accommodations were arranged far enough in advance so that she could travel with me.

Her trip intrigued my friends and at Philadelphia Airport on that cold Friday evening in December many of them showed up to see us off. All bon voyage parties are fairly similar, but this send-off was an exception, especially when the two of us arrived with a caravan of luggage. At least I could be seen. But Betté-lu was in her travel case, which was decorated with Christmas wrapping and a big red bow on the handle. However, in spite of all this attractiveness, Betté-lu rebelled.

Howling and clawing—anything to get out—she made quite a racket. I never realized she has such a strong pair of lungs. I tried to look around nonchalantly as though I had no idea where the noise was coming from.

She had to be in her box in order to be weighed in with the rest of the baggage. In the box she weighed 14 lbs.—and at the cost of two dollars per pound. The protests coming from Betté-lu did not endear me to onlookers, some of whom appeared to be thinking in terms of the S.P.C.A. The airline people were not too happy either, and in the middle of the confusion I remembered that I had forgotten my driver's license. All in all, it was not one of the most propitious departures.

In due course, we were aboard the plane, and from the very beginning she took an intense interest in the proceedings. As soon as we were airborne I opened the travel case and placed her on the seat next to me, alongside an Englishman by the window, whose eyebrows arched at the sight of her. More startled than disturbed, he smiled, and I was relieved. (I could have been given a seat next to a cat hater.)

Betté-lu's new red collar and leash (travel regulations also) didn't seem to bother her; nor did she seem to mind the pretty stewardesses stopping by to pet her, and she took a definite fancy to the captain, who greeted her in passing.

That morning I had fed her early but then not for the rest of the day. I had lined her travel box with paper and some litter, just in case. However, she didn't have to go all night which was a blessing. It may also have had something to do with her delicacy in these matters, which is human. She insists on complete privacy.

During the movie I dozed off. I was awakened by two light paws on my leg. Everyone was asleep. Only a dim light came from the ceiling. Betté-lu was standing up, glancing up and down the aisle, wondering why it was so quiet and what had happened to all the people. She looked at me full of questions.

I whispered to Betté-lu that people were sleeping, and I was relieved that she didn't even let out a meow.

She was a marvelous companion. If you were at all timid about flying, her calm curiosity would make you forget the imaginary pitfalls and dangers that plague the mind.

Whenever I had to visit the powder room the Englishman would hold her leash, and all the while she'd keep a watchful eye down the aisle till she saw me returning. Both at dinner and at breakfast Betté-lu never once tried to sniff my tray—which does at least prove home-training is important.

At 8:15 A.M., we touched down at Heathrow Airport in London. It was a mass of rain and sleet, with a terribly heavy fog.

Into her travel case went Betté-lu. The two of us were the last to leave the plane. Then down the steps and onto a bus that was to take us to the Pan Am terminal.

As I sat down in the bus with my hand luggage and the cat's box at my feet, a man suddenly approached.

"You are the lady with the cat?" he asked.

"Yes . . . , " I answered tentatively.

"Then you are to come with me," he said. "There's a special car for you and the cat, to take you over to BEA terminal for your flight to France." Those seated near me heard this and stared.

"Well now," I smiled, "it looks as though we're really going to have a royal welcome." (I was wrong—but let's not get ahead of the story.)

I was told to board the plane again and wait for the car. As soon as I did, I let Betté-lu out of her travel case. Her yowls from inside the case seemed louder, maybe because she was getting lots of practice. There were some seedless grapes on a dish, left over from someone's breakfast. I opened some and gave them to her. The poor thing was so hungry by this time she could probably have eaten her leash.

A half hour had passed before a motorcycle finally drove up, and a man wearing a helmet marked "Police" came aboard. He handed me what seemed like a hundred papers to sign, all pertaining to the complete history of this international cat.

He told me that a car was coming to take me to the BEA terminal and the cat to Her Majesty's SPCA, where Betté-lu would be examined and fed, and there she would stay till it was time for our departure to Nice.

This was upsetting news. I told the officer that my brother had been waiting for me at the Pan Am terminal since 8:15. It was then 9:15.

"We shall notify him to meet you at BEA," he said. "We're frightfully sorry for the delay, but we have rather rigid government regulations concerning all animals brought into the country.

"The cat, I'm afaid," he continued, "must come with us and not stay on with you. Otherwise, she'll be placed in quarantine, which used to be six months and just recently has been extended to eight."

I sat speechless.

"This is why you're not permitted to go to the Pan Am terminal. You are in transit enroute to France, and you are to be taken directly to BEA, where you'll catch your flight."

At this point I was too exhausted to argue with Her Majesty's policeman.

By this time, the car that was to take Betté-lu and me to our respective quarters had arrived. I tried to hold back my surprise. For outside waiting for us stood a gleaming Bentley with a uniformed chauffeur beside it.

"Now I know the Queen likes cats! Imagine—sending her limousine to escort us!" I bubbled. The chauffeur stood unmoved.

Betté-lu, of course, just stared. Her only reaction came when I placed her back in her case. Then she started howling most unroyally and protested bitterly all the way.

My only concern was that nothing should happen to her. I envisioned Grandfather's reaction if something should go wrong. I decided to drop a hint.

"I hope that cat will be with me when I arrive in Nice, or my family will cause an international incident!"

"Oh, but of course!" the policeman said. "You can be certain she'll be on that flight."

As soon as I arrived at the BEA terminal I headed for the powder room. I felt I really needed a warm bath and a bed at this point, having travelled all night and changed time zones.

When I finished trying to make my face look alive, I heard my name called out over the loud speaker—I was to report to the Information Desk. There I was told to go to the Entrance Gate, where my brother was waiting for me.

The reunion with my brother and his wife was a relief for all of us. Naturally, the moment we saw each other our faces lighted up. But as we approached the gate from either side,

At London ... waiting for us at the foot of the plane's steps
stood a Bentley with a uniformed chauffeur to take Betté-lu to
the Royal SPCA.

two customs officers stopped us.

"You can't go through, madam! You're *in transit!*" That phrase again.

I stared at them. "Then please let my family come inside here."

One man shook his head adamantly. The other said, "I'm afraid they can't. This section is for flight passengers only!"

"But I haven't seen my brother in two years," I exclaimed.

"Frightfully sorry, madam."

"Can't they just come inside till plane time? We've so much to talk about."

"I'm afraid not, madam."

I felt my face redden.

I noticed that everyone I had encountered so far seemed "terribly afraid" or "frightfully sorry." Of whom or what, I wondered. They used these terms in every sentence. Well, by God, I would let them know I wasn't afraid, and I spoke up. "What are we supposed to do? Stand here for another hour and a half talking through a gate?"

The officer shrugged his shoulders. "You go through that gate, madam, and your cat will be quarantined for eight months."

After several moments of feeling like an absolute failure I reacted as any red-blooded American would.

"No wonder our ancestors broke away from this country! This is another Berlin Wall!"

All the while my brother and his wife were being charming diplomats, telling me not to get upset, that you can't buck the British because they're first and best in everything. (I was never before so proud that I was a DAR.)

I ignored their calmness and raised my voice to the customs officer. "You could at least supply us with chairs. We can't just stand here. My brother is just out of the hospital, and we ladies aren't up to it."

The officer didn't move.

Finally, all this fencing became too much for me. "In America," I said, "ladies are always given chairs. When your British women come to our country they find that our men are gentlemen."

The officer put down his papers and pencil. He stood up and called across to a man fifty feet away. "Randy, bring three stools over here."

He turned and looked squarely at me. "I'll show you that we treat ladies as well as your American men."

I winked at my sister-in-law, who is from Vienna. She just smiled wanly and bit her lip.

Within a very short time we three were seated on stools five feet apart, talking through the gate as people noisily passed through. As a result we had to shout at each other just to be heard. Of course all the passersby could hear our conversation too. How cosy it all was!

"I wish I could at least treat you to a cup of coffee," Allan remarked. "It's awful—your first trip to England and we can't entertain you. All because of a cat! Besides, we don't even get to see this animal. What in heaven's name does she look like?"

"She must be an exceptional cat," said Judy, "to have such an expensive trip."

For the first time in my life, I thought perhaps I was out of my mind.

Here was the famous "London Town" I had always hoped to visit. And I could have had an excellent chance to see everything and stay as long as I wished, except that at this moment Betté-lu was controlling my life. Astrology revealed in

"You are in transit, Madam! You go through that gate, and your cat will be quarantined for eight months!"

my natal chart that I'm a child of destiny. After this, I thought, I'll never disbelieve it.

Our reunion was anything but what we had hoped for. But it gave us a lot of laughs, at least in retrospect, we'll long remember.

An hour later we said our farewells, and I promised that on my return trip nothing would prevent me from visiting them, nor from seeing Stratford on Avon—a schoolgirl dream of mine.

Finally, I found my way to the BEA plane to Nice. I stood there at the boarding steps and looked around. I raised an eyebrow.

"Where's my cat?" I asked a stewardess. "She's supposed to be here with me to go to Nice." I wasn't taking any further chances.

"Oh," she said, "*you're* the lady with the cat. Well, she's already aboard, and when we arrive at Nice you'll have her."

I swallowed, and not knowing what kind of red tape somebody might come up with next, I said, "I want to see the cat, and I want her with me."

"I'm afraid you can't," said she. "It's not regulations. She must ride in the freight area."

I then asked to see the captain of the plane.

A quick discussion took place between the stewardess and an officer, after which the captain came to the doorway and down the steps to me.

"I'm frightfully sorry, madam, but our regulations are that all animals must fly in the freight area."

"But she sat next to me from Philadelphia to London——"

"Yes, I know," he said, "but that was Pan Am. BEA is different. Animals cannot be free on the plane. I'm afraid she can't even put a paw down. If she did, she'd be on British soil and would be quarantined for eight months."

This tight little island was getting tighter by the moment.

Then I explained to the captain that I was concerned Betté-lu would take cold, that I wanted her in good health when we arrived in Nice. He assured me he'd personally see that she was properly cared for.

I went aboard, reluctant but at the same time glad that I was getting nearer to our destination.

It was only an hour and a half trip to the Riviera, and as we flew up and away from the fog and sleet, I welcomed the thought of the beautiful warm sunshine of the Cote d'Azur.

Not until we arrived and I was going down the steps of the plane did I see Betté-lu, cradled comfortably in the arm of the captain as he held her travel case in the other.

He gave me a warm smile. "I kept her with me in the cockpit, to be sure she wouldn't take cold."

Instead of being annoyed Betté-lu seemed perfectly contented, wagging her tail, delighted to be free of her travel case and basking in the warm air and sunshine.

I apologized to the captain for being upset.

He patted her head affectionately.

"Reminded me of when I was a bomber pilot in the war. I owned a black cat named Churchill that I took with me on every mission. He brought me luck."

I picked up Betté-lu and we went off together to the French Porte d'Entrée, expecting a similar ritual of examinations, doctor's certificate and another hundred papers to sign.

When we came to the gate, I handed my passport and Betté-lu's vet certificate to the French officer. He looked at Betté-lu in my arms, gave her a Gallic wink and said, "Me-ow." Then he stamped my passport and handed it back to me, and not looking at the health certificate at all, he

I could have taken an elephant into Nice, and they wouldn't have said a word. Vive la France!

smiled and said, "Entrez, Madame. C'est notre plaisir!"

I was flabbergasted. I could have taken an elephant into France, and they wouldn't have said a word. Vive la France!

I caught a glimpse of the family in the distance. They were glad to see us both. However, Grandfather seemed more taken up with the welfare of Betté-lu than with me. This gave Mother and me a chance to talk in the taxi on the way to their apartment on the Promenade des Anglais.

Of course, I told them of the British accommodations for Betté-lu, of my exceptional visit with my brother at the gate and of the cat's journey in the cockpit. It seemed amusing to relate, and it amused everyone I encountered thereafter. In theory, perhaps, this is why I began to write this story.

It was two weeks before Christmas. As we drove along the coast from the airport along the palm tree lined Promenade des Anglais, it was somewhat hard to believe that only an hour and a half before, we had been in snow and sleet. Nice—the Eternal City of Flowers—lives up to its name.

Places were already colorfully decorated for the holiday. And traffic was heavier than usual, as the winter season was beginning again.

When we reached No. 147 Promenade des Anglais, the concierge, Monsieur Charbonier, was at the door to greet us. He was an Algerian, whose eyes were black and round and whose plump cheeks shone like apples. Seeing Betté-lu he raised a gentle eyebrow. "Ah, la petite chatte. Elle est très jolie!"

The French are said to be distant with foreigners, but I urge you not to believe it. That Frenchman took to Betté-lu like a long lost love. Such a fuss he made—offering to get her some food and some milk. Not only was our cat invited into the concierge's quarters, but before her visit was over she paid social calls to almost every apartment in the building.

As for hospitality, I believe it has been said that it is easier for an American to gain admittance to the drawing rooms of Buckingham Palace than to have lunch with the French in their homes. Betté-lu broke through the barrier. She was cordially received for both luncheon and dinner by everyone.

It has also been said for centuries that every man has two countries, his own and France. Betté-lu set out to prove it.

The French like cats; it's a fact. And for them, this Yankee cat was different. People thought her "American accent" was charming. Personally, I couldn't see the difference. The sound of her me-ow was the same to me as any other cat over there. But if they found la différence—all the better. For it made life more comfortable and more fun for all of us. Through her we met many people I don't suppose we would ever have known.

The only time I sensed Betté-lu's nervousness on the whole trip was when we went up in the open elevator cage through which you could view the marble staircase circling it. Her eyes were tensed, and her claws cut through the fabric of my winter coat. She seemed relieved when the elevator reached our stop—the cinquième étage which was actually the sixth floor. (The French never count the ground floor as the first.)

As soon as we entered the apartment I put Betté-lu down on the floor, and for several moments she stood in the middle of the mirrored foyer, gazing about her strange new home. After a short inspection she followed her great pal, Grandfather, into the kitchen, where he had fully prepared a welcome for her. He had bought several cans of French cat food, a box of their biscuits and some milk, as well as a bag of litter and a green pan for her personal business.

After sniffing the food, she would only drink some milk, in spite of her long fast since leaving Philadelphia. However, heaven only knows what Her Majesty served her in London.

It is small wonder that she scorned the French food. It didn't come in liver, fish and chicken flavors like the Friskies she adored. Later, after she learned to like champagne, caviar, and other such goodies, she still returned to Friskies with a hearty appetite. At least she never ordered hamburgers at Tour d'Argent.

After her small meal Betté-lu followed us on a tour of the apartment. And when we went from Mother's bedroom out onto the balcony overlooking the beautiful blue Mediterranean, Mother picked her up and cuddled her like a long lost grandchild.

From the night of her arrival Betté-lu chose to sleep in the kitchen on the marble floor, which was very warm from the heating pipes beneath it. She never used the basket that had been purchased for her at the Galeries de Lafayette—the only thing French she did not take to.

After dinner that first evening we all sat restfully in the salon near the open French doors, looking out at the passing ships, lighted like Christmas trees, sailing out from the harbor towards the sea.

Betté-lu was nestled beside Grandfather on the sofa. Her head was on his lap, her eyes half closed in that delicious repose only a cat seems able to achieve fully, and his hand stroked her soft fur.

I shall conclude this part of my story by saying that Betté-lu was at peace again. Her family once more was all around her. And from that moment on we all settled down to live in the French way.

The morning after our arrival we people needed no alarm clock to awaken us. Betté-lu emerged from the kitchen and went from bedroom door to bedroom door me-owing at us to get up at seven o'clock. This was something she had never done before.

Evidently she had slept well and was fully acclimated to the five hour change in time. I wasn't. I was exhausted and could have slept for two days. However, the early reveille that began that morning persisted every morning thereafter, in spite of our protests. It has now become a 7 A.M. ritual. No matter where she lives or in what time zone, at 7 A.M. she's full of pep and in perfect voice.

Betté-lu's morning meows are a subtle blend of greeting and impatience. She seems to be saying that she disapproves of our laziness at that fine hour of the day, but that she's willing to overlook it if we all get up without further delay. Faced with a choice between getting rid of Betté-lu or agreeing with her, we get up.

The social life in our apartment building was governed by our neighbors, who came mostly from the north of France.

On the ground floor on either side of the marble entrance hall, were people who owned their apartments and had beautiful gardens in the front. Both families loved their pets so much that they wanted them to have the freedom they had had in their homes before coming to Nice.

One neighbor was Madame Renault and her daughter Marie Françoise, who soon became Mary Frances to us all. She enjoyed hearing her name pronounced the English way.

Mary Frances was a professor of English at the Université de Nice. Their permanent home was in Dijon near the Swiss border where the darling mustard pots are made. Mme. Renault was in her seventies and the widow of an Army colonel. There was also a son, a doctor still living in Dijon at their family chateau, who came for a visit while I was there. It was their tomcat, Mistée, who fell in love with our Betté-lu.

Our neighbors on the other side of the main entrance on the ground floor were the André Moreaus, who owned a country house at Fontainbleau and an apartment in Paris as well as the one in Nice. Monsieur Moreau was ninety years young and had a chic second wife. "Young" is the only way to describe M. Moreau, for his mind was as alert as if he were forty. His charm and wit were the same. It was only his legs that were feeble from poor circulation. However, daily before lunch he could be seen crossing the Promenade on his canes and strolling up and down the tile walkway in front of the apartment building. Then he'd rest on a bench for awhile and begin again. He spoke English quite well. He had been a banker in Paris and had visited America many times.

Monsieur Moreau had had all sorts of animals in his lifetime, but at the moment he had only a parrot called Philippe. Philippe was a prize pet whose domicile was a hundred-year-old red and gold Chinese cage which stood in their salon.

Philippe was shocked when he first saw Betté-lu, and he protested loudly—in French, of course. He was so hostile, in fact, that we had to make great efforts to quiet him. Betté-lu remained wide-eyed the whole time. Madame Moreau said it was only jealousy on Philippe's part, and then she began making a fuss over him.

Her soothing words brought amazing results. Thereafter, with very good manners, Philippe would greet the cat warmly with a "Bonjour, Betté-lu," or "A bientôt, Betté-lu."

Betté-lu loved to spend an afternoon or evening at the Moreaus'. They would always arrange to have broiled chopped sirloin for her, served in a special dish in the kitchen.

M. Moreau was certainly the kindest of men. He loved to

Philippe would greet the cat daily with a "Bonjour, Betté-lu."

talk and reminisce about his visits to New York and our other cities. He spoke warmly of the many wonderful things he had found in America, from the generosity of her people and their potential for good, to the New York Stock Exchange, to our American bacon. M. Moreau liked bacon so much that I brought him a pound of Oscar Meyer's finest on a previous Christmas visit. I had traveled by ship, and the bacon had been kept in the ship's refrigerator. In the bustle of disembarking I forgot about it, until the captain tapped me on the shoulder and ceremoniously presented me with the package, neatly tied in a festive red ribbon.

Then there were M. et Mme. Pinson from Metz, who lived on the same floor as ours. They had a canary who wouldn't sing. They made great efforts to learn the cause and spent a vast sum of money with voice instructors. But to no avail.

One day when our front door and theirs happened to be open at the same time, Betté-lu ventured out across the hall and into their apartment. I chased after her. And suddenly she was running at top speed, darting wildly from room to room through the stranger's apartment meowing as she went. I finally retrieved Betté-lu from under the woman's bed and returned with her, jabbering my apologies. This catastrophe became a miracle. Their canary, seeing the chase of the cat and hearing her squeal, broke out suddenly into perfect voice and sang beautifully.

Thereafter, Betté-lu was invited to "chez Pinson" often, and we were permitted to come along, too.

After two weeks I came to realize that Betté-lu's only outings were on the balconies of our building. She had not yet set foot on French soil. Having gone through that ordeal in

Grandfather and Betté-lu strolling on the Promenade des Anglais.

England I felt she should put her paw down on the "pays d'amour."

Of course, if you thought she could go out alone on the Promenade you're wrong. The traffic was always racing by as though every French driver were rehearsing for the *Grand Prix*. The beaches always had several dogs climbing about the rocks. And then, too, I wasn't certain how she'd take to the sea.

So one day, Grandfather picked her up, leash and all, and carried her to the street. Mother and I stood on the balcony looking down. We watched them as they emerged from the main entrance. Monsieur Charbonier, the concierge, stood talking to them for a long while. I thought he'd never stop petting Betté-lu.

Finally, Grandfather set her down and began walking. Betté-lu revolted. He picked her up and walked a few feet, and then he put her down again. Still she wouldn't budge. No doubt the traffic and noise and all the strangeness frightened her. Grandfather picked her up again and, looking up at us, motioned that he was taking her across the Promenade to the beach.

Perhaps some cats like water—a little, anyway. But with a whole big sea for her to play in, she squealed in protest.

I hurried down with the camera and found Betté-lu in tears, crying and howling hysterically. I had never before heard of a cat that cried, but poor Betté-lu was weeping as though her heart would break. Whether the breeze was responsible for her tears I do not know, but when I petted her affectionately, reassuring her of my love, they stopped. When she seemed fully relaxed again I snapped her photo.

After this unsuccessful episode we didn't attempt to take her to the beach again.

Madame Pinson's canary broke out suddenly into perfect voice.

The Christmas season was an exciting time. Our neighbors had visits from all their various children and grandchildren from the north of France.

Everyone was very nice, inviting us to their festive celebrations. Also, the people in our building had friends in the other apartments along the Promenade. It was one social call after another. It was at Mme. Renault's New Year's Eve party that Betté-lu formally met Mistée, the big, golden tomcat. A short time after the guests arrived, Mistée, who had been placed in the garden, happened to look through the French doors and discovered our shy and gentle Betté-lu. The old French cat almost flipped. Just looking through the windowpane he fell madly in love with our little American queen.

I never saw such swooning. Mistée actually begged for Betté-lu's attention. His openly amorous tactics stopped all conversations, and the guests stood watching his floorshow. He'd bounce against the French door, scratching the windowpane. Then he'd leap backwards and turn himself over and squirm. Then he'd return to the window glass and stand there meowing at the top of his lungs.

Betté-lu looked at this old man as though she thought he had lost his mind. And from that moment on poor Mistée was never the same. He pined away, pressing his face against the glass for glimpses of La Belle Dame Sans Merci.

One day about a week after New Year's I decided to take Betté-lu to Cap Ferrat, to the villa I owned and had lived in with her old friend Pepper so many years before. I couldn't bring myself to go there during the holidays because of so many memories, especially now that most of the family had passed away.

Monsieur Moreau had offered to take us in his new Citroën.

Of course I thought his chauffeur Raoul would do the driving. But when we got into the back of the car, M. Moreau was seated behind the wheel. Then Raoul got in and sat next to him.

I thought it was a joke, considering he was ninety years old, and that he would turn around to me at any moment with a witty remark and change places with Raoul. But M. Moreau turned on the ignition and put his foot on the accelerator, and the car started to move forward.

We were all more than a little worried. For the best part of the way we were plunged into deep silence. Betté-lu, who sat on my lap, didn't move a muscle.

We drove up the Moyene Corniche and around those hairpin curves past Ville Franche. The traffic was extremely heavy. The only sound was Raoul's voice: À gauche—à droit—lentement—*arrétez*—allez—*à gauche*—à droit." Somewhat surprised, we arrived at the villa safe and sound.

As we turned into the pebbled entrance drive I felt a lump form in my throat. We parked in the circular drive alongside of the fountain where my marble statue of a boy holding the horn of plenty still stood.

My thoughts flashed back quickly to the afternoon my father-in-law took me for my first glimpse of the villa he was giving us as a wedding gift. It's a peach colored house with a lovely flower garden, shaded from the glaring sun by tall cypress and palm trees. It lies at the far end of the family estate at the point of Cap Ferrat, where our closest neighbors were the passing boats in front of us. It is a charming two-story place with balconies, French doors and massive geranium vines covering its walls. It was a week after we moved in that my husband's grandmother bought the poodle for me at Monte Carlo; and it was with a happy heart that I carried home the little jewel.

When we got out of the car, M. Moreau sat down on a bench with Mother and Grandfather. He too had wanted to see the place we spoke of so often.

I carried Betté-lu in my arms and went inside. The house was so silent—I remembered following my father-in-law from room to room, hardly believing this home was to be mine.

The rooms were large with parquet floors upstairs and marble ones downstairs. Aside from the need of a coat of paint, the place had been well cared for by my former tenants, who had moved to Tangiers a few months before.

I wandered slowly through the rooms, gazing at the furnishings, remembering the joys and the sorrows of life at Cap Ferrat. As the years mounted my life had risen to a state of turmoil; and it may be difficult to imagine how events could have changed so—how I became so sick with sorrow and uncertainty that I was forced to leave this beautiful home.

After our tour of the house I put Betté-lu down, and we took a stroll through the garden. I remembered the day I spied Pepper, feasting on an old bone, and how it had given me the greatest delight to see him drop his meal to run and greet me.

As Betté-lu followed me down the gravelled path I could see her old friend Pepper running ahead, sniffing the velvet grass, broken twigs and fallen flower petals. I could still hear his voice, which mirrored his moods in a wide range of inflections. Listening to us, he had even learned to "sing"—a series of soft and loud tones accompanied by eyes sparkling with fun. He got so that, in a playful mood, he performed on request to "Sing, Pepper."

When we came to the clearing at the end of the path, Betté-lu and I stood there, looking out at a passing boat and at the beautiful sea.

To some a dog is simply an animal, but when I was feeling low-spirited and despondent, my little friend's warmth and

Betté-lu stood on the cliff at Cap Ferrat looking out at the passing ships just as Pepper had done many years before. . . .

affection toward me were almost human. There are some who'll say Pepper had no soul. But he had a heart and he knew whenever I was terribly unhappy.

As Betté-lu meowed and rubbed against my sandal, I remembered the last night I had stayed at the villa.

It was a time of mental agony and loneliness. Pepper and I had been seated on a rock, and without his little yelps and comforting presence I might have done something drastic. The edge of the cliff seemed very near, and the prospect of a quick descent into oblivion, in which I would forget and be forgotten, was inviting. While an animal is not to be compared with a human being, their absolute trust and love have kept more than one person from forgetting that there is something to be said for going on with living.

It was after this episode in the garden that I took Pepper home with me to Chestnut Hill, where he later became little Betté-lu's playmate.

I looked down at Betté-lu, and saw that she was watching me intently. As she looked up into my face, tears formed in her eyes. It was probably the wind off the sea, making her eyes water. But I am an incurable romantic.

Finally, after a memory-filled visit to the cliff with Betté-lu I picked her up and walked back to join the others. I found them in a corner of the rose garden, bent over what I thought was one of the special rosebushes. Instead, I found that they had discovered Pepper's old friend, Hubert, the family turtle. I thought it must be a mirage.

My own eyes grew misty, seeing my initials still plainly inscribed at the base of his shell. On the last trip I made to Nice I hadn't seen him and had thought he found another home. I put Betté-lu down and held her by the leash. She stared as only a cat can stare.

It was a great meeting. Betté-lu made several attempts to touch the turtle with her front paw but quickly retrieved it. Curious but cautious, Hubert tucked his head back into his shell and sat there like an ornament. Betté-lu stiffened. She stood like a statue. Then her tiger-striped tail began to turn like a propeller. She meowed in frustrated rage, thinking this strange creature was trying to pull something over on her. I scolded her and explained to the others Hubert's long-time friendship with Pepper. It may have been my frequent mention of "Pepper," but whatever the cause her stare turned to a sympathetic look and her tail stopped winding. After a few moments of stillness, Hubert stuck his head out again, and we all rejoiced.

When we drove away from the villa I felt somewhat contented to know that there was still a member of the household looking after this place.

A few days later Betté-lu received her very best surprise. We had discovered a fabulous mall recently opened at St. Laurent Du Var, a few kilometers from the Nice racetrack. It's very similar to the malls in America, with a large variety of shops and one big supermarket. This new place had stocked various American groceries. But the one which gave Betté-lu the greatest delight was her ever-loving Friskies.

Naturally, we bought a carton of each of the ocean fish, liver and chicken varieties, and when Betté-lu heard the sound of her old familiar box rattling, her eyes danced with joy. Of course, we sent several boxes downstairs to Mistćc, who lovingly devoured them—I suppose because they were from Betté-lu.

The two cats saw each other frequently, and always Mistée

would put on a little floor show—trying to entice Betté-lu. However, after two months of this Mistée became ill. And after a period of only a few days he died of heart trouble. (More than anything else I was certain that Mistée's new romance in his autumn years had been too much for him. But I kept that thought to myself.)

Mme. Renault and Marie Françoise were greatly distressed over their loss, and they came to look forward to Betté-lu's company more and more.

Meanwhile, I was making my plans to leave Nice and return to America with a stopover in London. And this time, I was determined to have a real visit with my brother and his family. However, child of destiny that I am, fate always seems to step in.

It was the day after the Mardi Gras celebration that altered my plans. We had enjoyed carnival week on the Riviera with its many parties before the Lenten season. We had watched the parade of decorative floats passing by the apartment building. We had invited the neighbors to come up and see the fabulous fireworks from our high terrace.

Grandfather was out taking a morning stroll on the Promenade, when he slipped and fell on the curb, striking his head and eye. Monsieur Moreau saw it happen and got hold of some people to help Grandfather back to the apartment.

For several hours, poor Grandfather screamed in pain, yet he refused to have a French doctor. He wanted only his American doctor three thousand miles away. He would not be comforted, and his agonized protests became more and more violent.

Mme. Renault came up and washed out his blood-swollen eye. Mother tried to reason with him, telling him that he was in no condition to take a plane back to America, which was what he wanted to do. Besides, she told him, there were many wonderful French doctors available.

He continued to protest at the top of his voice until M. Moreau suggested a Docteur Michel—Jean Michel, a noted eye surgeon on the Riviera. The name Michel worked like a miracle. Grandfather had at one time owned a favorite kitten called Michele. This name seemed to calm his fears of French doctors, and finally, he agreed to see him.

Grandfather's fall was serious. The injury was fatal to the eye. The surgeon ordered him immediately to his own eye clinic at St. Roche's Hospital in Nice. The eye had to come out.

However shocked we were, Grandfather agreed with his diagnosis and went along with him calmly. The following morning Dr. Michel removed the eye successfully.

On the day of Grandfather's hospitalization, Mme. Renault offered to take in Betté-lu as her guest while we were going back and forth visiting him. It was there that Betté-lu really took on the French way of life and heard only the French language spoken.

It was at Mme. Renault's that she learned to eat raw eggs. The famous brown egg, which is only served in France and other continental countries, appealed to her appetite. She never cared for our American white eggs. Yes, she subscribed to the theory of the French—that the brown egg has more protein than the white egg.

By the time we rescued Grandfather from his buxom, doe-eyed, vivacious French nurse at the hospital (but that's another story), Betté-lu had become perfectly at home staying with Mme. Renault and Marie Françoise. Of course, just so she wouldn't get homesick, she had taken her own wardrobe with her—her red collar and leash, and her own household things—litter pan, bed and blanket and bowls.

Mme. Renault said she was honored to have our cat as her guest, especially now that Mistée was gone. But I think Betté-lu is the one who should feel honored. After all, how many American animals—two-legged or four-legged—are even invited to live for two weeks in a real French home, and a palatial apartment at that, on the Riviera?

It became apparent that life with these two lovely French ladies left an imprint on Betté-lu. Ever since she has had a certain air about her. She seems to strut now with a "look who I am!" expression written all over her. Even her meow now sounds different to me. She has definitely become a Continental.

After Grandfather came home to the apartment his convalescence was slow and difficult. The loss of his eye made him very sensitive. In fact, at first he didn't want to wear a black patch over it, even though it was a temporary thing until a plastic eye could be set in.

Realizing his sensitivity I made a big thing out of the black patch. I recalled to him famous men like Lord Nelson and Stephen Girard and John Wayne, who even won the Academy Award for *True Grit*.

"And look at General Dayan of Israel," I told him. "He defeated the Egyptians in six days, wearing a black patch. Imagine what he might have done if he had both eyes! Besides," I continued, "women seem to go for men who wear a black patch. There is something mysterious about them."

In spite of this, Betté-lu seemed to be the only one who could comfort Grandfather. All my quips meant nothing. She spent her days and nights in his bedroom. When he was well enough to get up, she'd guard him on his canes.

43

To our sorrow, when Easter came, Grandfather began to suffer from vertigo and nausea. Naturally, we feared there might have been a head injury in the fall. Next he felt an occasional numbness in his left arm and leg.

During this critical period he thought his time had come and wanted to be taken back to America to die. And when Dr. Michel brought in a general surgeon, Dr. Cier, to see him, and they recommended that he return to the hospital for further tests, Grandfather rebelled.

"My God," he said, "France has my eye now. They're not going to get my head. I want to go home!"

Grandfather was now ready to draw up his last will and testament. Instead, however, arrangements were made to bring him home to America on the SS *Raffaello*.

It was decided that Betté-lu would travel on the ocean liner, too. Her ticket read like any other passenger's, but again she had to go through the requirement of a physical check-up by a vet.

I must say Betté-lu didn't seem the least bit upset about this the way she had been the night I took her to the vet in Chestnut Hill. In fact, she rather enjoyed it.

I still remember how she gracefully walked into the Clinique Vétérinaire at 30 Rue Verdi, holding her head high and giving a look of approval when she met Dr. Rombi, the French vet. Naturally, this is what she wanted—to be able to tell her cat friends back home that she had had her very own French doctor, too, just like Grandfather.

By now Betté-lu was a French linguist (especially after her stay at Mme. Renault's). And her green eyes actually danced when the vet said to her, "Viens ici, ma petite chérie. Vous êtes très jolie!" I don't mean to brag, but Betté-lu stood there on his table like a soldier while he examined every inch of her and gave her a vaccination shot.

On the way back to the apartment we stopped at the Negresco Hotel and had some tea and pastry on the terrace. Betté-lu, who loves formal tea parties, sat beside me nibbling on her own tarte aux pommes. This was another reason she loved France. Animals of any size or shape, color or breed—so long as they're on a leash—are very freely allowed in the restaurants and hotels. They are accepted as people—more so than French children, who are disciplined severely. Certainly, Betté-lu was "people," but she was not a provincial. She was treated as a person of international rank, and she loved it.

Finally, after the many days of packing our five trunks, fourteen suitcases, and one cat travel case—with its Christmas wrapping still intact—and all last minute items accomplished, we were ready to sail for America. We hated to leave our many lovely friends, hated to leave this beautiful corner of the world, but, knowing it all so well and having visited there so many times in the past we were certain to return again someday. The bon voyage champagne party that M. et Mme. Pinson gave us in their apartment was a memorable evening. Of course, their canary was there and sang beautifully. Everyone was enchanted by the sweet tones of this golden prima donna and equally amused by the story of Betté-lu's squealing, which had first given the canary her voice.

However, the high point of the soiree was when Betté-lu meowed and smacked her lips, making no attempt to conceal her desire for some champagne—a taste she had acquired in the recent months. So without hesitation, a small crystal glassful was placed on the parquet floor for her, along with a small dish of caviar. She sipped casually and ate as daintily as a French debutante. Afterwards, she purred affectionately.

Our French neighbors, I am certain, will long remember Betté-lu and hold her in high esteem.

Late the following day we went in a hired limousine to Cannes. In spite of the five trunks already transported earlier in the week, I didn't think we'd all fit in. With the suitcases, the cat and the three of us—twenty-three pieces in all—we looked like an advertisement on the problems of ill-planned tours.

Later, much to my distress, standing there on the dock at Cannes, my thoughts flashed back for a moment. And I remembered bringing Pepper to America for the first time, on the S.S. *Independence*. Here I was again, this time bringing home Pepper's little friend Betté-lu on her first ocean cruise.

It was turning dusk when finally we walked slowly down the wooden passageway towards the tender with the cat leading the way—just as Pepper had done many years before. The bright lights of the *Raffaello* anchored in the harbor reflected an impressive painting on the smooth water around us. It was the same kind of beautiful evening, with almost every star shining from the heavens.

The rumble of the motor and the movement of the small boat caused the cat to tremble just as Pepper had, and she squirmed close to me on the bench. I cuddled her tenderly under my arm, and then I looked towards the shore and the dim lights of Cannes, thinking of the way experiences repeat themselves.

The captain and his officers stood in formation at the lower opening of the ship, cordially greeting the fifty-two passengers from the tender.

At the far end of the line was a white uniformed steward who reached out and took the cat's leash from my hand.

"Signora Contessa," he said, "your cat, please. I am Alberto, in charge of the kennel on the Lido deck. She will be well cared for there. You may see her as often as you wish from eight in the morning till seven at night. Now, may I ask her name?"

"Betté-lu," Grandfather spoke up. "It's Betté-lu—see that she eats no starches or sweets."

"Sì, Signore," answered Alberto, "grazie." Then he bent down and stroked the cat's head. "Molto bène, Betté-lu, come along. I've been expecting you."

Leaving Betté-lu in Alberto's care, we took the elevator to our staterooms, which were next to one another on the foyer deck. After we had rested and bathed we went to the dining room where we were given a choice table facing the entrance; it was interesting to watch the guests come and go.

Instead of looking over the other passengers and enjoying the delicious cannelloni all'Emiliana, poor Grandfather's only concern was Betté-lu. He wondered what she was eating. He retired early. And yet, I knew he wouldn't be able to sleep, but would lie awake worrying about his cat.

Bright and early the next morning, just as the ship was approaching Naples, I took Grandfather up to the kennels. There were seven dogs and four cats of all breeds, each in his own cage, yelping and meowing.

I spotted Betté-lu. Alberto was feeding her. He stopped his work at the sight of us.

"Buòn giorno," he smiled. "Your cat, she is enjoying the voyage."

When Grandfather saw her devouring the lobster in her dish, his face lighted up. Then when he saw the small blanket in her cage, he was fully contented. Betté-lu was certainly travelling first class—and at the cost of only $10 for her boat ticket.

Other passengers who had pets came and went, but Grandfather was different. Every morning he'd walk her up and down the Lido deck. People were amazed how supremely happy Betté-lu was with her red collar and leash. She became the talk of the ship. In fact, she hit the headlines three days later.

Just three miles outside of Gibraltar, a British tanker struck the bow of the *Raffaello* at four o'clock in the morning. The damage was serious, and the ship had to return to Gibraltar for repairs. The Associated Press came aboard, for this was News. Everyone's thoughts went to the ill-fated *Andrea Doria* of many years before.

The Press toured the *Raffaello* and in time discovered Betté-lu, strolling with Grandfather without a care in the world. Their cameras filmed her, and overnight she became a celebrity.

In the days following the shipwreck Betté-lu was greatly disappointed that she couldn't visit the wild monkeys of Gibraltar.

Ironically, of all the ports in the Mediterranean where the ship might have been repaired, Gibraltar is a British colony. And there again to step upon Her Majesty's soil would only mean another quarantine as in London.

"Certainly not," I protested for Betté-lu. "Not again!" This time we accepted her fate gracefully, and every morning she could be seen peering through the railing on the Lido deck, looking the town over and gazing up at the ancient rock of the Moors.

"After all," she might well have purred, "how many cats get

At Gibraltar Betté-lu stood on the Deck staring up at the "Rock," pondering the legend of the wild monkeys.

a free week like this—with the compliments of the Italian Lines."

We soon found out that Betté-lu's trip abroad had given her an insatiable thirst for knowledge. After our daily excursions into the town we always sat up on her deck with Betté-lu tied to my chair. She seemed to listen intently as we talked of our impressions of this or that tourist spectacle. She was especially attentive when she heard us speak of how the barbary monkeys of Gibraltar had turned the tide of the War. Legend says that while these monkeys remain, Britain will continue to hold the Rock.

Of course, people smile at this. Yet during the War, when the number of monkeys and Britain's fortunes were dwindling simultaneously, no less a person than Winston Churchill issued orders for the maintenance of the monkey contingent. As their numbers were built up, Britain's fortunes turned.

The experience of cruising proved relaxing for Betté-lu, too. Every day she basked in the sunshine and ate continuously, just like the rest of us. She proudly meowed and walked about the deck like all the other passengers aboard.

A week later, as we were docking at New York, I watched in surprise as Betté-lu picked up the handle of her leash and held it in her mouth. American flags were flying, and in the distance strains of "The Star Spangled Banner" could be heard. Her tail waved joyously, as if she were convinced this celebration was in honor of her homecoming. (Had she looked at a calendar, she would have learned it was Memorial Day.)

Nevertheless, she was now ready to disembark. She knew we had reached America, and she was happy to be home.

At New York . . . Betté-lu picked up her leash as "The Star
Spangled Banner" was played.

It was just a short time later that Betté-lu was back in her garden at Chestnut Hill. There she was, a gentle and sophisticated international lady, telling all her neighboring friends about her exciting winter on the French Riviera.